VOLUME 2:

inspirational
quotes FOR
meaningful
moments

D1257532

PUBLISHER: Autumn Leaves
COMPILED BY: Erin Trimble
BOOK DESIGN: Crystal Folgmann

For information about bulk sales or
promotional pricing, please contact:
Autumn Leaves
4917 Genesta Ave.
Encino, California 91316
1.800.588.6707
www.autumnleaves.com

ISBN 0-9761251-0-2

Designing With...
A Division of Autumn Leaves
Encino, California

Printed in Canada